THE SILVERTOW
LETT

Gerard Melia

HODDER AND STOUGHTON
LONDON SYDNEY AUCKLAND TORONTO

British Library Cataloguing in Publication Data
Melia, Gerard
The Silvertown letters.
I. Title
822.914 PR6063.E4/

ISBN 0-340-42358-7

First published in Great Britain 1988

Typeset in Monophoto Lasercomp Bembo by Cotswold Typesetting Ltd, Gloucester
Printed and bound in Great Britain for Hodder & Stoughton Educational, a division of Hodder and Stoughton Limited, Mill Road, Dunton Green, Sevenoaks, Kent by Richard Clay Ltd, Bungay, Suffolk

Note to the Teacher

Silvertown Letters is a development of two previous plays based on the same theme. Newham Teachers' Workshop presented *Silvertown 1917* in a variety of venues throughout East London in 1975, including Colleges of Education and, subsequently, Loughborough University. A professional company, Soapbox Theatre, produced a rewritten version of the play called *Shellshock* in schools and arts centres throughout the South East.

This particular version was written for the Newham Theatre Workshop in 1984. It was performed at the Tom Allen Arts Centre, Stratford and at the Half Moon Theatre, Mile End.

The idea for the play arose from the need to present local history within a community, to help people to identify with the past and to inform new generations of the joys and struggles of living in Dockland.

Thames TV used a novel based on the same materials in their programme *Middle English* as an example of how pupils can use the resources of the Local Studies Library for creative writing.

As with all books in this series, suggestions for classroom use and production can be found in the accompanying support material.

Gerard Melia
February 1988

List of characters

Harry
Bill
Conductor
Winnie
Alfred
Molly
Louise
Stanley
Mrs Snellgrove
Photographer
Journalist
Grandad Snellgrove
Elsie
Mrs Lacoste
Jeanette Lacoste
Mrs Jackson
Mrs Bailey
Mrs Claridge
Mrs Perry
Bert
Miss Moore
Vicar
Mrs Burford
Editor
Reporter
Posh Lady
Constable
Sergeant
Orderly
Nurse

Various soldiers, children, policemen and men and women at First Aid Station

THE SILVERTOWN LETTERS

Scene i

[*The trenches in Flanders, 1916. The intermittent roar of a shell barrage is heard. Two soldiers are heard singing dispiritedly.*]

I don't want to be a soldier
I don't want to go to war
I'd rather stay at home
About the fields to roam
And live on the earnings of a lady typist.

I don't want a bayonet in my belly
I don't want my buttocks shot away
I'd rather be in England
In Merry Merry England
And rusticate me bloomin' life away.

[*Shells whine overhead and crash quite near.*]

HARRY: It's three days now. When do you think our lads will give Gerry his share?

BILL: Haven't you heard, mate? We've run out of shells. We haven't got enough shells. Look, mate . . . I came from Blighty six days ago, right? Listen what Kitchener – Lord Kitchener – told the newspapers . . . I've got my copy here . . . it's got the wedding photograph in as well see . . . that's the Mrs. . . . the one wearing the veil, right? That's her sister Winnie . . . she's only twelve. Smart kid . . .

Anyway, over the page, column two, there you are . . . see. [HARRY *strains to read in the dim trenchlight.*] Oh, sorry mate, I forgot . . . well, it says: 'Unless the whole nation co-operates in supplying the necessary arms, ammunition and equipment, successful operations in the various parts of the world in which we are engaged will be very seriously hampered and delayed . . . it is absolutely essential that the arrears in the delivery of our munitions of war should be wiped off.'

[*More shells whine overhead and explode.*]

HARRY: Well, what's happening? . . . Who's going to do something about it? . . . I mean, it's bloody stupid . . . Whoever heard of a war being fought without bleedin' ammunition?

BILL: Just keep your head down and keep praying they miss, matey.

[*Shells explode around them.*]

Scene ii

[*Thames at North Woolwich. Sounds of river traffic and an approaching tram. The tram stops and the* CONDUCTOR *calls out:*]

CONDUCTOR: Terminus. All change. Woolwich Ferry – Woolwich Ferry. Come on you two. Mind the steps with that basket, Winnie.

WINNIE: All right, Mr Colclough . . . I can manage. Our Alfred's come with me tonight. Me Dad doesn't like me coming on me own.

CONDUCTOR: He'll protect you against all dangers . . . won't you, son?

ALFRED: Yes, Mister.

CONDUCTOR: How old are you then?

ALFRED: I'm eleven.

WINNIE: Next week . . . he's eleven next week. On 21 June. And I'm twelve . . . I'm two years older than 'im.

CONDUCTOR: Only twelve. Well . . . I thought you were older than that . . . And congratulations, Miss. Your Dad told me the good news. I'll bet they're all pleased in the fire station aren't they?

WINNIE: Yes . . . we're all pleased. I'm the first person in Silvertown to get a scholarship to Stratford East Grammar School.

ALFRED: She's the first.

CONDUCTOR: I know . . . I know . . . Is your sister working a double turn again?

ALFRED: She's making shells.

CONDUCTOR: I know what she's doing!

WINNIE: Yes. There's been a big order or something . . . I think they call it a 'push'. They've got to make hundreds of extra shells for the battle in France. So I bring her dinner in a basket and give it to her on the Ferry and she goes back to Woolwich without getting off.

ALFRED: She's going yellow . . . on her face.

WINNIE: It's through packing the shells. They use picric acid and they go yellow.

ALFRED: She couldn't get it off for the wedding.

WINNIE: Yes she did . . . well, nearly.

CONDUCTOR: The Ferry's coming in now, Winnie. You'd best get down there.

WINNIE: Right. Come on, Alfred.

ALFRED [*running to keep up with* WINNIE]: I can protect you . . . you know. I'm not stupid.

WINNIE: It's all right, our Alfred . . . I feel very safe with you around. Look, there's the girls. Wave . . . Molly! . . . Molly!

[*As the ferry draws near the girls from the day shift are singing off-stage. The song is 'Daisy Daisy' but they've changed the words.*]

Girlie Workers
Give us a hand here do
We're all busy
Sending shells to Crewe

We stuff 'em at Woolwich Arsenal
Where we make up a bloody great parcel
To be sent to Fritz and Wilhelm and Spitz
And one for Kaiser Bill's castle.

MOLLY [*shouting*]: Hallo, Winnie love! What is it?

WINNIE: Chicken.

MOLLY: Not again.

ALFRED: It was either that or corned beef and you said you were fed up with that.

MOLLY: Oh God. I see you brought the truth machine.

ALFRED: I'm protecting her.

MOLLY: Good lad . . . providing the attacker isn't more than four foot high,you'll be a big asset. Any letters . . . any letters from my Bill?

WINNIE: No, I didn't see any.

ALFRED: They only come from France on a Friday. You know that very well. Why do you keep looking for letters when you know they only come on Fridays?

MOLLY: Thanks, love.

CONDUCTOR [*in the distance*]: Come on girls. [*He rings the bell.*] I've got to be in Stratford Broadway in thirty minutes or I'll get the sack.

MOLLY: Run kids . . . or you'll miss the tram.

WINNIE: Cheerio, Molly.

ALFRED: Now remember . . . your letters come on Friday.

[*The tram clangs and moves off. The girls are singing again. The song 'Daisy Daisy' fades into the sound of marching feet and rain. Spotlight finds* WINNIE *standing downstage. She pulls out a letter and reads it.*]

'Dear Mr Mayor, Now that the War has been going on for two years, don't you think it would be a good idea to organise a Festival. Something to cheer up the people of West Ham is now necessary. It could take the form of bands and a circus and a week's holiday from school for all the children so they could take part in processions and everything. Perhaps His Majesty the King could be invited down to open it. Then afterwards everybody would be happy and smiling while doing their war effort. Please reply to the above address. Yours hopefully, Winnie Snellgrove.'

Scene iii

[*At the front. In the distance can be heard the occasional shell and explosion. As they march,* BILL *and his mate* HARRY *talk and share a bottle.*]

BILL: Pity about Lieutenant Perry.

HARRY: Bad luck. Must have been the last shell . . .

BILL: No chance.

HARRY: No, not a chance. Two splinters right through his chest. He knew he'd copped it. Asked for a fag . . . I refused at first . . . you know . . . our instructions, like . . . particularly with chest wounds.

BILL: You did right, mate . . . a couple of puffs at a fag wouldn't kill him.

HARRY: He went a bit funny, like . . . you know, in his posh voice.

BILL: Oh yeah.

HARRY: As he sat there he starts talking in a kind of mocking way about the commander.

[*A voice in the distance calls 'Halt'. The troops stop. Then the voice calls 'Right turn' and 'Fall out'.* BILL *and* HARRY *sit by the side of the road and pull out fags and light them.*]

BILL: Hold your hand still, son . . . how can I light me Woodbine with the bloody match moving about?

HARRY: I'm perished, matey. [*They both take deep drags and exhale. They share what's left of the bottle.*] Great! I needed that.

BILL: What did Lieutenant Perry say, Harry?

HARRY [*mimicking Lieut. Perry in a posh voice*]: You see, soldier, it's very simple. The Germans are entrenched over here. I want to advance here . . . and here. I bombard the ground here and around the trenches there. Bombard for several days. I thus indicate to my opponents, the Germans, my next point of attack. My troops dig in and wait. [*changes to his own accent*] That's you and me, soldier. Got it so far?

Good. Good. [posh voice] We shell and shell till I'm convinced there's not a single German left in the opposing trenches. I now blow my whistle and over the top we go. Straight into the shell holes filled with mud and water created by our bombardment. The German machine gunners now emerge from the deeper fortified trenches to which they have retreated untouched by our barrage and systematically annihilate the British troops – that's us – as we stagger and slush along towards them. Then what's left retreats . . . and we start all over again.

BILL [*laughing*]: It's funny isn't it . . . but it's bloody true.

HARRY: He gave me his St Christopher medal.

BILL: A gesture.

HARRY: Sort of swop for the fag . . . but he even joked about that . . . he said St Christopher was a good protector for journeys but it was now apparent to him that if you stopped still for half an hour the protection didn't work . . . then he died.

[SOLDIER *comes along delivering mail from home.*]

SOLDIER: Private Adams.

BILL: That's me, son.

SOLDIER: One for you. London postmark.

HARRY: From the Mrs.

BILL: No . . . not her handwriting . . . [*He opens envelope.*] Good God, it's from little Winnie . . . that's my sister-in-law. Very neat writing I must say.

HARRY: Got a fag?

BILL: Yeah, here you are . . . now listen to this. [*He reads the letter aloud to* HARRY.] 'My dear brother-in-law Bill, my teacher, Mr Sadler, says I should practise writing as often as possible. He thinks letters are a good way of expressing our thoughts and that sharing our thoughts is good for other people. He says it's a kind of written conversation. How are you?'

[*A shell whistles overhead and explodes nearby.*]

HARRY: Tell her to tell Mr Sadler we're just about doing all right at the moment.

[*Another shell passes overhead and lands very close.*]

BILL: 'How are you? Alfie and I take Molly's dinner to the Ferry every other day. She says she's very tired but glad to be helping in the war. Alfred would like to know when you fire one of our Woolwich shells. He says you can tell they're from Woolwich because they've got a yellow ring on the bottom.'

HARRY [*as a shell passes overhead*]: Can't see any yellow rings on that one, Bill, old mate. They're a bit quick for me.

BILL: Just shut up and listen . . . [*he reads letter again*] 'Mrs Jacob in Fisher Street has taken in some lodgers since her husband died.'

HARRY: Aye aye . . . is that what they call it down your way?

BILL [*still reading*]: 'They are from Belgium. Very nice, but they don't speak English very well. Molly's friend, Louise, she wasn't at the wedding because her father was in hospital in Preston.'

HARRY: Where's that then . . . Preston?

BILL: In Lancashire.

HARRY: Lancashire, eh? Well.

BILL [*resuming the reading*]: 'which is in the North.'

HARRY: Correct . . . 'cos you just said so . . . and she just said so . . . so it must be . . . in the North. Right?

BILL: Right. [*reading*] 'Her boyfriend, Arthur, has just got a job sorting out the stores at Brunner Mond.'

HARRY: Brunner Mond? Funny name.

BILL [*reading*]: 'at Brunner Mond factory. It has been empty for years and the Government has taken it over. It's something to do with shells.'

HARRY: Great . . . well they can send a few over here, quick.

BILL [*reading*]: 'We've heard there'll be plenty of jobs there next month . . . Mother and Father are doing well. Dad is now the senior fireman at Silvertown because he passed an exam last month. Alfie says to ask you is it true Kaiser Bill wears a helmet with a spike on the top when he's in battle. Have you seen him yet? Yours faithfully, love, Winnie Snellgrove.'

[*Fade to . . .*]

Scene iv

[*Children playing in the street. They chant a skipping song.*]

Kaiser Bill went up the hill
To conquer all the allied nations
Kaiser Bill came down the hill
And split his dirty combinations.

Kaiser Bill he didn't like
The way our Tommies knocked 'em down
He jumped on a bus and in a rush
He dropped a bomb on Silvertown.

ALFRED [*talking whilst the skipping game continues*]: That's stupid, that is. Don't you think that's stupid, Stanley?

STANLEY [*a boy of his own age.*]: What?

ALFRED: How could Kaiser Bill catch a bus from Germany to here?

STANLEY: I don't know.

ALFRED: Why drop a bomb on us anyway?

STANLEY: There's the docks, and the ships.

ALFRED: But we live here. They don't bomb people in houses, do they?

STANLEY: Why not – we're the enemy.

ALFRED: Stanley, you're dafter than you look. The Germans are the enemy. We're British.

WE ARE THE BRITISH

[*Sung by the children*]

Left, Right, Left, Right
Left, Right, Left, Right.
We are the British and we're going to win.
We keep on fighting through thick and thin.
We are the British and we're going to win.
We keep on fighting through thick and thin.

Don't like the Kaiser,
Don't like the Germans,
Don't like the Jerries
Or the Krauts.
We're going to beat them
We're going to bomb them
Out of their homes
And out of their trenches
Show them how the British boys fight.
We are the ones who are right.

We are the British and we're going to win.
We keep on fighting through thick and thin.
We are the British and we're going to win.

We keep on fighting through thick and thin.

[WINNIE'S MOTHER *comes to the door of her terraced house, carrying a pie, and shouts:*]

MRS SNELLGROVE: Winnie! . . . Winnie! . . . Come along now, dear . . .

WINNIE [*running*]: What do you want?

MRS SNELLGROVE: Take this hot pie to No. 18. Mr George isn't too well today. It's his back again.

WINNIE: Oh, Mum . . . can't our Alfie go . . .

MRS SNELLGROVE: His name is Alfred . . . you call him Alfred . . . madam. And don't argue with me. Just get down there and give it to him.

WINNIE: But, Mum . . . he smells.

MRS SNELLGROVE: So would you . . . you saucy madam . . . if you were 82. Now, do as you are told.

WINNIE: Oh, Mum . . .

MRS SNELLGROVE: Just do as you're told.

[A REPORTER *and a* PHOTOGRAPHER *are walking along the street looking for No. 12.*]

PHOTOGRAPHER: I suppose this street is typical of the area. I'll get a good shot in this light if they co-operate. There's No. 12. I'll set up my tripod across the street, all right?

JOURNALIST: Right, Sam. I'll do the talking.

MRS SNELLGROVE: Now, don't just stand there. Get going. That pie will be stone cold.

JOURNALIST: Excuse me.

MRS SNELLGROVE: Yes?

JOURNALIST: I'm Roland Smith. I'm looking for No. 12 [*he checks his papers*] – a Mrs Snellgrove and her family.

MRS SNELLGROVE: Yes, that's me.

JOURNALIST: Well, I'm from the Stratford Park Gazette. You sent your name in for our family feature.

MRS SNELLGROVE: Family what?

JOURNALIST: Our family . . . er . . . column. You know, we photograph a typical family from an area of West Ham and then we tell their story. You wrote to us and said you'd be willing to take part.

MRS SNELLGROVE: I never wrote anything.

JOURNALIST: Well, here's your letter.

MRS SNELLGROVE: I never wrote that . . . that's not my writing . . . my God . . . I know whose writing that is . . . Winnie! . . . Winnie! . . . just you come back here, madam!

[*Lights fade and* WINNIE, *stepping forward, reads one of her letters.*]

'Dear Sir, I would like to inform you of the wonderful work of our fire brigade at Silvertown. It is called a sub-station because it only has a few firemen. But it is the best fire station in West Ham because the Chief Fireman, who is my Dad, passed his exams last week. He got more marks than any other fireman and must therefore be the best. The public can be assured that any fires that break out down here in the docks will be put out very quickly. Yours faithfully, W. Snellgrove.'

Scene v

[*Lights come up on* MRS SNELLGROVE *arranging the photograph.*]

PHOTOGRAPHER: Come on now, ladies and gentlemen . . . don't be frightened by the camera . . . the flash won't harm anybody. Come on, Mrs Snellgrove, surely you don't mind sitting in the front.

MRS SNELLGROVE: Oh no . . . Oh no . . . I couldn't. No, let Grandad or our Elsie have a go.

PHOTOGRAPHER: It's only a photograph, Mrs Snellgrove.

MRS SNELLGROVE: Yes, I know . . . but all West Ham will be looking at me by Friday and I haven't done me 'air.

GRANDAD SNELLGROVE: I suppose I'll have to show the way as usual . . . these young 'uns don't have my sense of adventure . . . not like when I was young.

WINNIE: You sit next to me, Grandad.

GRANDAD: That's my girl . . . you show this lot how to behave.

ELSIE: It's her bleedin' fault we got to have our photographs taken. Her and her bloody letters, she should be stopped.

MRS SNELLGROVE: Let's see . . . who's missing? There's Elsie, father, Winnie, Alfred, Mrs Burford and our Bert.

ALFRED: What's she doing here? Nosey Parker.

WINNIE: She's like the weather, she gets everywhere. Look at her . . . ferret face.

MRS SNELLGROVE: Our Arthur – that's me husband – is on duty. He's a fireman.

PHOTOGRAPHER: Now, if you'll just sit in the middle, Mrs Snellgrove, we'll be ready.

[*Enter* MOLLY *and* LOUISE *from work.*]

MRS SNELLGROVE: Just a minute, there's Molly and her mate Louise. Come on, girls. Get your photos took quick. They works at the Brunner Mond now. They used to work at Woolwich.

ALFRED: Yes, they used to be yellow when they came home. Now they're white again.

MRS SNELLGROVE: Shut up, Alfred and fold your arms. Everybody fold your arms.

MOLLY: What's it all about?

MRS SNELLGROVE: For now just sit on a chair – you [*to* LOUISE] . . . and smile when he tells ya. Right? Just a minute . . . just a minute. Winnie, what's that you've got in your 'and . . . it's not . . .

WINNIE: It's the pie for Mr George.

MRS SNELLGROVE: Oh my God! The poor man. It'll be stone cold. Put it under the chair out of the way. Right, mister. That's about it, right?

PHOTOGRAPHER: Look this way, ladies and gentlemen – don't look at the flash. Look at me . . . now smile . . . come on now, smile . . .

[MRS LACOSTE – *the Belgian lodger – and her* DAUGHTER *enter, speaking in French. They disrupt the photograph.* PHOTOGRAPHER *re-assembles the family pose.* GRANDAD *puts his foot into the pie which* WINNIE *has left by his feet.*]

Scene vi

[*Four neighbours,* MRS JACKSON, MRS BAILEY, MRS CLARIDGE *and* MRS PERRY, *enter and watch the photograph being taken, from a distance.*]

MRS JACKSON: Well . . . well . . . that's a fine thing I must say.

MRS BAILEY: What? What's a fine thing?

MRS JACKSON: Them. Why them? Why should they have their photo taken?

MRS BAILEY: There's no telling these days. It's the war what does it.

MRS JACKSON: What? Does what?

MRS BAILEY: Changes people. Makes 'em suskeptable.

MRS JACKSON: Makes 'em what?

MRS BAILEY: Makes 'em suskeptable . . . they do things what they didn't expect . . . like having your photo took.

MRS JACKSON: In the street . . . not in the privacy of your own home . . .

MRS CLARIDGE: Away from prying eyes.

MRS PERRY: You can tell she's had a hard time with that lot . . . she lost her first two you know . . . both boys . . .

MRS JACKSON: Like I said at the time . . . she couldn't carry boys . . . some women can't you know.

MRS BAILEY: What?

MRS JACKSON: Don't you listen proper? . . . carry boys . . . they can't carry boys.

MRS BAILEY: But she had her Bert . . . he's there, look . . . isn't he hers? . . . I didn't think she'd adopted any.

MRS PERRY: She had him normal.

MRS CLARIDGE: Well, yes . . . but look at 'im.

MRS PERRY: Been difficult 'as he?

MRS CLARIDGE: Nearly lost 'im three times . . . didn't think they'd rear 'im . . . small . . . thin . . . a decent gust of wind and they've got to peg 'im down . . . [*she giggles*]

MRS BAILEY: No! . . . You're not serious?

MRS JACKSON: 'Course not you silly bugger . . . he just hangs on to something.

[*They all laugh, but stop when* MRS SNELLGROVE *appears to be looking at them.*]

MRS PERRY: Her husband's a fine man.

MRS BAILEY: One of the best.

MRS PERRY: Sat all them exams for firemen . . . and passed.

MRS BAILEY: Strange though.

MRS PERRY: What's strange?

MRS BAILEY: Having to pass a test to put a fire out.

MRS JACKSON: God, you're stupid . . . you need all that information – like reading maps – so as you can find the fire, and writing . . . writing down how it happened and who was burnt . . .

MRS PERRY: I fancy that assistant of his . . . the one with the blonde hair and big feet. Very sort of eye-catching . . . very . . .

MRS JACKSON: Some people's interests are very low, very low indeed.

MRS BAILEY: Really? . . . Oh!

MRS JACKSON: Oh, what?

MRS BAILEY: Well . . . er . . . I think he's nice as well.

MRS PERRY: God . . . this war's got a lot to answer for. Oh dear [*looking at* GRANDAD]. What's happened to Grandad?

MRS CLARIDGE: What's the matter now?

MRS BAILEY: Her father don't look much.

MRS CLARIDGE: Not long for this world is Grandad.

MRS JACKSON: Won't see the year out.

MRS CLARIDGE: He's a good sort, though. Very kind to them Belgiums and always ready to help a mate.

MRS JACKSON: He's been the strength in that house.

MRS CLARIDGE: Yes, I suppose he 'as. Her husband working shifts and everything.

MRS JACKSON: He's got a bad habit . . . this habit . . .

MRS CLARIDGE: A habit? . . . Is it a *peculiar* habit?

MRS JACKSON: Spitting – tobacco spitting – he sort of aims at things and brags about it . . . hitting 'em from ten yards away. Their back door down the yard is stained . . . stained with his . . . competitive instinct?

MRS PERRY: Oh, I thought you meant habits with . . . women.

MRS JACKSON: No . . . he's past all that . . .

MRS PERRY: That Winnie is strange . . . strange and quiet.

MRS JACKSON: Deep waters.

MRS BAILEY: Deep waters run silent.

MRS JACKSON: 'Course they do, you silly cow . . . but I know what you mean.

MRS CLARIDGE: This business of writing letters . . . can get out of hand.

MRS BAILEY: How do you mean?

MRS CLARIDGE: Information!

MRS BAILEY: Information? . . . I don't understand.

MRS CLARIDGE: Revealing important things to the enemy.

MRS BAILEY: Has she written to the Kaiser then?

MRS CLARIDGE: Could have.

MRS JACKSON: Why not? The little bugger has written to everybody else. She wrote to our Edwina . . . she's in the same class . . . 'on your reply' she says 'pretend you're a war widow'. Well, I mean to say, our Edwina hasn't even started her . . . you-know-whats yet . . . how would she know about being a widow. Bit early at twelve for that kind of thing.

MRS PERRY: As for Molly . . . well . . . a real forward madam she is. Changes her job more times than her underwear if you ask me. A quickly flashy smile at the foreman and she gets the job easy . . . without qualifications.

MRS BAILEY: Is she a bit . . . you know?

MRS PERRY: Wouldn't surprise me . . . even though she is a married woman.

MRS JACKSON: He's at the front . . . fighting.

MRS PERRY: She's very ambitious . . . and cheeky. Them things don't go together if you want to get on.

MRS BAILEY: You've got to be prepared to serve haven't you? You've got to smile a lot . . . to get on, I mean.

MRS JACKSON: You could smile till your teeth fell out, love . . . you're married, so that's it for you, my gel . . . don't you be getting ambitious, all right?

MRS BAILEY: All right . . . Can't I dream a bit?

MRS JACKSON: 'Course you can . . . while you're doing the washing . . . 'course you can, gel.

Scene vii

[*The parlour of the Snellgrove house. The family are having tea and biscuits whilst the* JOURNALIST *questions them.*]

JOURNALIST: Now, Mrs Snellgrove . . .
MRS SNELLGROVE: Well . . . I'm mother of this lot. [*they all laugh*] I don't go out to work except Saturdays, when I

does laundry at two big houses in Forest Gate. Looking after this lot is a full-time occupation. We don't want for much 'cos my husband, Arthur, got a good job at Silvertown Fire Station. That's just three doors away on the corner. You passed it on your way here.

JOURNALIST: Yes, I saw it. It's not very big is it?

MRS SNELLGROVE: Well, it's really a sub-station – but there's six men there . . . and they're always ready . . .

JOURNALIST: Yes, all right. Now, who else have we here?

BERT: I'm Bert Snellgrove and next week I start work. I've got a job as a clerk down the road at the rubber works.

GRANDAD [*laughing*]: It's not much of a job. The rubber works only pays its workers when they remember.

ALFRED: And it smells worse than Mr George at No. 18!

MRS SNELLGROVE [*gives him a smack*]: Don't you talk like that, Alfred. This is Alfred. He's very bright, and he's in Standard 5 at school. He missed Standard 4 because he was clever, didn't you, Alfred?

ALFRED: Yes.

[*There's a pause because they all expected* ALFRED *to elaborate, but he doesn't.*]

JOURNALIST: The two young ladies?

MOLLY: I'm Molly. I'm married. My husband's at the front.

ALFRED: She means he's in France – not out in the street . . .

JOURNALIST: Yes, I understand.

MOLLY: I used to work over at Woolwich but the overtime and the work got me down so I got this secretary's job to Dr Everett at Brunner Mond.

JOURNALIST: That's where they make explosives now?

MOLLY: Official Secrets, Mister. I'm not allowed to confirm or deny.

LOUISE: It don't matter no-how . . . we're finishing on Friday.

MRS SNELLGROVE: Finishing? Finishing? What do you mean, gel?

MOLLY: We're fed up with it.

ALFRED: I'm fed up with Sunday School.

MRS SNELLGROVE: You've only been there three weeks.

LOUISE: It's Brunner Mond . . . it's too bloody dangerous for me. It could go up any day.

MOLLY: Dr Everett knows it's dangerous. They send him letters to tell him so and I know 'cos I'm his secretary, aren't I?

ALFRED: At Sunday School Miss Moore says it's wrong to read other people's letters.

MRS SNELLGROVE: Miss Moore is right . . . you shouldn't read private papers like that . . . you could go to jail for that.

ALFRED: See! I told you!

MRS SNELLGROVE: If you tell anybody what you read in them letters you're a spy.

MOLLY: Don't be stupid, I ain't telling anybody anything . . . anyway, I'm leavin' . . . Louise and me has got ourselves a couple of jobs in the canteen at the Premium Flour Mills . . . down West Silvertown . . . we start a week Monday . . . now come on, Mum, concentrate on your interview.

[JOURNALIST *sings following song. The rest of the cast join in.*]

YOUR COUNTRY NEEDS YOU

Family feature, photographs, local news,
Talking to the people, hearing all their views,
Women, children, toiling in the factories,
Making shells, There's going to be some casualties.

The generals they all say
'The Germans they must pay'.

They've no time for regulations, safety rules,
No concern for our relations, they're just tools.
Grey streaked hair and yellow faces
Going through their dangerous paces.

Your duty you must do,
Your country needs you.

[*Fade to . . .*]

Scene viii

[*Tramp of soldiers' feet and the sound of distant shell fire. The soldiers are whistling the song 'It's a long way to Tipperary'.*]

HARRY: Where the hell is Tipperary?

BILL: In Scotland . . . or somewhere like that.

HARRY: Are you sure?

3RD SOLDIER: No he's not sure, mate . . . not unless the Kaiser has shelled that as well and moved it. Tipperary is in the South of Ireland.

HARRY: Well, it is a long way from Leicester Square then?

3RD SOLDIER: At this pace it's three weeks away from London.

HARRY: And a swim.

BILL: Thought it was in Scotland . . . I thought they made that special whisky the toffs drink – malt whisky . . . sure it was in Scotland.

HARRY: No, it's Ireland . . . I remember now . . . there's a fella in Canning Town . . . keeps a pub . . . name of Paddy Fallon . . . he comes from a place called Kilkenny and I remember him saying that Tipperary was next door, so to speak . . . definitely Ireland.

BILL: Are you sure?

HARRY: Sure . . . Here's the rain again.

BILL: I'll bet it always rains in wars.

HARRY: No, it don't . . . not always. Kitchener didn't get much at Khartoum, did he?

BILL: All these shells whistling through the air spoil the weather . . . if they'd stop for a month I'm sure the weather would pick up.

HARRY: The weather doesn't 'pick up' anywhere in November.

[*A barrage of shells whistles overhead and explodes quite near. A second wave is heard briefly and explodes among the marching soldiers. Screams and groans of the injured and the sound of running feet as other soldiers come to help the wounded.*]

VOICES [*off-stage*]: Stretcher bearers . . . stretcher bearers . . . over here . . . Sergeant, detail them men to cordon off the area . . . Help that man, soldier . . . don't just stand there staring. That's no use to him. Who's got some shell dressings? Quick man, over there, he's still alive.

[HARRY *has been seriously injured.* BILL *has been wounded by a shell splinter in the leg.*]

BILL: Come on, mate . . . come on . . . you're not bad are you?

HARRY: It doesn't look so good.

BILL: Come on, sit up, Harry . . . let me get my arm around your shoulders . . . that's it . . . now, come on, sit up.

HARRY: Shell, wasn't it, Bill?

BILL: For sure . . . sure it was.

HARRY: Next letter you write to that kid in Silvertown . . . tell him it didn't have a yellow line on it . . . so it wasn't 'from Woolwich . . . got a fag? . . . it's allowed. There's nothing wrong with my chest . . . it's the bottom half what got it.

BILL: 'Course, mate . . . here . . . [*He cries out in agony.*]

HARRY: What's up, Bill?

BILL: The bastards . . . they got me too. My leg's bleedin' . . . and me hip . . .

HARRY: Give us a fag, mate.

BILL: What? . . . Oh yes . . . here you are . . . Harry? Harry? Here's your fag. [*He offers it to* HARRY, *who doesn't move.*]

ORDERLY [*comes and looks at* HARRY]: Sorry, soldier . . . he's had it . . . let's have a look at you . . . that's not bad . . . not too bad at all . . . that's a good blighty passport, soldier. You won't die, laddie . . . it's a job for the surgeon, then blighty for you.

[*Fade to . . .*]

Scene ix

[*The office of* DR EVERETT, *the Works Manager of the Brunner Mond factory.* MOLLY *is reading over a letter she has typed for him.*]

MOLLY [*reading the letter*]: 'Dear Doctor Freeth, The vacuum plant here at Silvertown has functioned efficiently and without any apparent signs of stress for eight months. By applying a vacuum to the liquid TNT the cooling consequent of this procedure has produced TNT of a very high quality and free from foreign and debilitating impurities. The only problem which causes me any real concern is the transport difficulties. Because of delays on the rail system – strange as it may seem we do not have a priority – we are forced to store more explosives than prudence and good management would allow. I fully appreciate your continued concern for our safety here in Silvertown. I do understand the dangers inherent in our process, but these are small when one compares them with the daily hazards of our armies at the front. This TNT is badly needed. What choice do we have? You and your colleagues should feel justly proud of your achievements in producing such a solution to the problem of producing more effective TNT. I hope the Managing Director up there in Cheshire appreciates your tremendous contribution to our war efforts. Best wishes, B. Everett.'

MOLLY [*continuing*]: Two p's in appreciate . . . yes . . . that's right. Well, Dr Everett . . . it might not bother you but I'm scared to hell . . .

LOUISE [*enters*]: Are you ready for home?

MOLLY: I'll just put this in an envelope.

LOUISE: Your escort has arrived.

MOLLY: Alfred?

LOUISE: Right first time . . . but he's brought the Silvertown correspondent with him.

MOLLY: Our Winnie?

LOUISE: Yes. And you're not going to believe it but . . .

MOLLY: It's not another bloody letter is it?

LOUISE [*nodding*]: Afraid so. And believe it or believe it not . . . the letter is addressed to Dr Everett.

[ALFRED *and* WINNIE *enter rather sheepishly.*]

MOLLY: Now, what's all this about our Winnie? What in God's name do you want to write to Dr Everett about?

[WINNIE *doesn't answer.*]

LOUISE: Will you read it to us?

[WINNIE *looks at* ALFRED. *He beckons her to one side and they whisper.*]

ALFRED: You want to bargain for your position.

WINNIE: What do you mean?

ALFRED: Tell them you'll only let them read it under certain conditions.

WINNIE: What conditions?

ALFRED: That you read it yourself and that they allow you to leave the letter on Dr Everett's desk.

WINNIE: Right. That's very good thinking. Thank you, Alfred.

ALFRED: Don't mention it. I know about these things you know. I've heard about unions and things. I'm very well up . . .

WINNIE: All right! All right!

MOLLY: Well, what's the verdict?

WINNIE: Well . . . I'll read it to you if you'll let me put it on Dr Everett's desk.

MOLLY: You read it . . . madam . . . and I'll consider whether it's sufficiently important enough to bother Dr Everett.

WINNIE: Oh, all right then. [*She opens the letter and begins to read.*] 'Dear Dr Everett, My letter will be quite a short one because I don't know you very well so I'll try to be very businesslike. All the factories in Silvertown make useful things. The Premium Mills make flour and bread. The Gutta Percha factory makes rubber cable. The Beckton Gas Works lights our streets and the Sugar Refinery makes syrup and jam. What do you make? It seems to me you make death. How can a clever man like you do such a thing? Wouldn't the war stop if one side had nothing to fire? I await your reply, Yours faithfully, Winnie Snellgrove (Miss).

[*Fade to . . .*]

Scene x

[*The Snellgrove home.* MRS SNELLGROVE *is washing the dishes.*]

MRS SNELLGROVE: Alfred! Are you there Alfred Snellgrove? Come in here this minute. [ALFRED *enters reluctantly.*] Grab that cloth and get drying these dishes. It's your turn. [ALFRED *does so.*] What do they teach down at that Sunday School, eh? Share and help . . . that's what they tells ya . . . share and help. God telling us all to help each other.

ALFRED: He's not helped me much . . . up to now.

MRS SNELLGROVE: God knows and see all things . . . even our most secret thoughts . . . I learnt that at school and it's very, very true. Them at that Sunday School ought to learn you that. Helping your Mother and Father is a commandment.

ALFRED: What about Stanley, Stanley Coster? He ain't got a father.

MRS SNELLGROVE: Well then . . . that's very hard . . . very hard that is. But Stanley helps his mother more . . . he stands in for his dad . . . in a manner of speaking. He'll grow up quicker – quicker than the likes of you.

ALFRED: I'll bet!

MRS SNELLGROVE: He gets the coal from the coalyard every Friday. He has an old pram. And he takes his younger sister to school and he does the shopping of a Saturday. You never help if you can get out of it. I'll have a talk to this Miss Moore. She should be telling you to help more at home.

ALFRED: Miss Moore is always saying that.

MRS SNELLGROVE: So she should.

ALFRED: I don't like Miss Moore. She talks as though God were a personal friend of hers . . . as though God would bother with the likes of her. She's got spots you know . . . on her neck.

MRS SNELLGROVE: That's enough of that nonsense.

ALFRED: Must I keep going to the Band of Hope?

MRS SNELLGROVE: Of course – you little heathen. And whilst I remember . . . that Belgium lady . . . Mrs Lacoste says you're to take her little girl Jeanette tomorrow. So don't you forget.

ALFRED: I'm not taking a girl so that's flat . . . [MRS SNELLGROVE *gives him a slap.*]

MRS SNELLGROVE: Just you do as you're told.

ALFRED: She won't know what's going on. She don't speak a word of English.

MRS SNELLGROVE: She can join in the clapping and the tambourine.

ALFRED: She's not having Winnie's tambourine.

[*Fade to spotlight on* WINNIE, *who reads the letter to the* VICAR.]

'Dear Vicar, at Sunday School last week Miss Moore

asked us to love our enemies. Does that include the Germans who are killing our men at the front? It did occur to me that perhaps a German vicar or was telling German children the same thing. Who is right in this matter? Yours faithfully, Winnie Snellgrove.'

Scene xi

[*Band of Hope tea party. Noise of children playing with whistles and balloons, etc.*]

VICAR: Appears to be going well, Miss Moore?

MISS MOORE: Oh, indeed it is, Vicar.

VICAR: What time are you expecting to finish?

MISS MOORE: Oh, in about an hour's time. We normally finish about 8 o'clock. We're going to start our sing-song. Would you like to start us off, Vicar?

VICAR: Oh no, Miss Moore. I'll leave that in your capable hands. Actually . . . I'm just going across to the Vicarage for an appointment with Mr Jepson. He promised to call in on his way from work. He's the engine driver from the Brunner Mond factory. His daughter is getting married next month and we're making the final arrangements. See you a little later, Miss Moore . . . perhaps you'd care for a cup of tea in the Vicarage later on?

MISS MOORE: Thank you, Vicar. I might be only too glad for a rest after this lot.

[*The piano starts to play the introduction to 'Hope the Hermit'.*]

Come on now, children – Hope the Hermit – you all know this one – you've learnt it at school I'm sure.

ALFRED: Come on, Jeanette, put that vase down. If you break it . . . [*she does*] Push the bits under that chair, nobody will notice . . . and stop crying . . . non-non-crying mon petite . . . non . . . me parley vous Belgium to you . . . non . . .

MISS MOORE [*singing*]:

Once in a blithe green wood
Lived a Hermit wise and good
Whom the folks from far and near
For his counsel sought
Knowing well that what he taught
The dreariest of hearts would cheer
Tho' his hair was white
His eye was clear and bright
And he thus was ever wont to say
Tho' to care we are born yet the dullest dawn
Often heralds in the fairest day.

ALFRED [*singing*]:

Tho' to care we are born yet the dullest dawn
Often heralds in the fairest day.

Jeanette, mind that glass with your feet!

MISS MOORE: Come on now everyone – second verse:

The very longest lane
Has a turning it is plain
E'en the blackest clouds will fly
And what can't be cured
Must with patience be endured.

VICAR [*whispering*]: Miss Moore . . . Miss Moore . . . have you a moment . . . it's quite urgent.

MISS MOORE: As cheaply we can laugh as cry.

Come on children, sing. Yes, Vicar, what's the matter?

VICAR: A fire has broken out near the Brunner Mond factory. It's quite a big blaze . . . if anything happened. . . .

MISS MOORE: Don't worry, Vicar. We're all right here . . .

Tho' to care we are born
Yet the dullest morn
Often heralds in the fairest day.
Tho' to care we are born
Yet the dullest morn . . .

[*There is a gigantic explosion. A gust of wind is followed by a second explosion and the roof and walls of the hall collapse. Children scream, some call for their parents.* MISS MOORE*'s voice is heard strong and clear.*]

MISS MOORE: Stand still everyone! Don't move. I'm holding a piece of the roof up with my hands. Those children near me can crawl behind me and go out through the door. Mrs Burford! . . . Mrs Burford! . . .

MRS BURFORD: Yes . . . I'm here.

MISS MOORE: Could you give me a hand with this roof piece? It's digging into my shoulder.

MRS BURFORD: Oh yes . . .

ALFRED: I'll give you a hand, Miss Moore but Jeanette, this Belgium kid, won't leave go.

OTHER CHILDREN:

I'm frightened. I want to go home!
My Mum won't like this. This is my best suit and I've only borrowed it for today!
My hand's bleeding, Miss Moore!
Miss Moore, get me out please – I'm stuck!

ALFRED: Oh shut up – she's doing her best!

VICAR: I've brought some help, Miss Moore – come on children, this way. [*He shines a lamp.*] Follow this lamp children. We'll soon have you out and in safety.

ALFRED: Eh you – follow that light – and push off – I'll take you home after . . .

CHILD: My leg's caught under this beam.

ALFRED: Mind a minute. Right – are you ready? I'll count three then you pull your leg out, all right? Right, one – two – three. [*He disturbs a crossbeam.*]

CHILD: I'm free . . . I'm free . . . but I can't move.

ALFRED: Where the hell are you? Reach out your arms and I'll try to find 'em – you bloody stupid . . .

MISS MOORE: Please mind your language, Alfred – now. Hurry children, I can feel the roof sinking. Vicar, Vicar, could you help me hold up this section?

VICAR: Of course, Miss Moore.

CHILD: Is our house all right, Vicar?

VICAR: I would hope so. Now, get along outside. [*to* MISS MOORE] Let me take the strain on my shoulders.

MISS MOORE: It's not going to matter much longer, the whole roof will go in a minute. Just get the children out – please!

VICAR: Of course, my dear . . . of course.

ALFRED: Give a hand here, Vicar. Shine that lamp. Thanks. Right, I can see you now, matey. Come on, let's have you out of there. I'll have to drag you. You're too big for me to lift.

VICAR: Good lad. Let me give you a hand. Fine. Come along now. Here we go. Right.

[MISS MOORE *screams and the roof falls in completely.*]

[*Fade to . . .*]

Scene xii

[*Noise of a fire engine arriving at the site of the explosion. Two policemen enter. One is a sergeant.*]

1ST POLICEMAN: Where's the Silvertown engine?

2ND POLICEMAN: Gone up in the explosion – can't find a single piece of it. The station has been blown to bits as well. This is a big bang, matey, I can tell you. Look over there. The Premium Mills is ablaze too. It's sprayed fire for over a mile around. Half the streets are wiped out. Get on the 'phone and get more engines from HQ.

[*Fade to . . .*]

Scene xiii

[*Newspaper office of local Gazette.*]

EDITOR [*speaking into 'phone*]: Yes I know there's been an explosion. We heard it here plainly enough in Stratford. Can you confirm it was Brunner Mond? . . . Good. I've sent a reporter down . . . what? He won't be allowed in the area? . . . Why not? There's nothing secret about this explosion . . . they've seen it on the terraces of the Houses of Parliament . . . that's plain stupid . . . anyway, I can't call my man back . . . he went half an hour ago . . . No, I will not submit my script to you. This is a matter of great public concern . . . [*He puts the 'phone down.*] David . . . David . . . get a photographer and get down to Silvertown. Harry went half an hour ago. Find him and get cracking.

[*Fade to* REPORTER, *Harry, arriving at the Band of Hope Sunday School.*]

Scene xiv

[*Band of Hope Sunday School.*]

REPORTER: Are you all right? Is there anybody underneath?

VICAR: Give me a hand. Miss Moore is just caught by the arm. Could you give us a lift just here? Thanks. [*They lift the piece of wood and release* MISS MOORE.] Careful, Miss Moore . . . careful.

MRS BURFORD: She's unsteady, Vicar. I think she's going to faint. [*She does.*] There, I knew she would. Been a terrible strain it has. I'll get her a cup of water. All right if I gets her a cup of water, Vicar, from your house?

VICAR: Of course.

REPORTER: I'm a reporter. Could I have your names, please!

MRS BURFORD: I'm Mrs Burford. I'm Miss Moore's assistant. I'll be back in a minute with the water. That's Miss Moore on the floor. That's the Vicar.

ALFRED: My name's Alfred. Alfred Snellgrove.

REPORTER: I know who you are, young man. We did a feature on your family didn't we . . . a few weeks ago?

ALFRED: That's right. Our Winnie wrote you a letter.

REPORTER: We won't forget that in a hurry. Are they all right?

ALFRED: Who?

REPORTER: Well . . . your family.

ALFRED: Why shouldn't they be?

REPORTER: Look . . . er . . .

ALFRED: Alfred . . . Alfred . . . my Mum insists.

REPORTER: Well, look, Alfred. This explosion is pretty big. It's affected a lot of streets.

ALFRED: Fisher Street?

REPORTER: I'm afraid so.

ALFRED: I see . . . I'd better get down there and give a hand to them.

REPORTER: You might be in the way. And there are soldiers and . . . sightseers . . . and reporters.

ALFRED: They'll let me through . . . I'm well-known around here. Anyway, my Mum will need me to help out.

REPORTER: But, Alfred . . . it's really bad.

ALFRED: We're tough in Fisher Street. Thanks – I'm off. If you see a little Belgium girl called Jeanette, look after her till I gets back?

REPORTER: Sure, I'll see to her.

MRS BURFORD: Right, here I am. I'm ready now. Fire away with your questions. By the way, my name's Burford – B U R F O R D. Burford. I'm 37 years of age and I live in Victoria Dock Road, No. 27. I've been with this Sunday School for practically 15 years. Well, you could say I've managed it virtually single-handed . . .

[*Fade to . . .. . .*]

MRS SNELLGROVE: Vicar . . . Vicar . . . 'as anybody seen the Vicar?

VICAR: Yes . . . yes . . . I'm here. Can I help?

MRS SNELLGROVE: Have you seen my Alfred? He came here to the party. He brought that little Belgium girl, Jeanette.

VICAR: The little Belgium girl is over there in the kitchen of the Vicarage . . . be careful . . . the explosion blew the garden wall over and what's left isn't very safe.

MRS SNELLGROVE: I was coming home from visiting friends in Forest Gate . . . I've run all the way . . . are you sure our Alfred's all right?

REPORTER: Hallo, Mrs Snellgrove . . . I'm very glad to see you safe.

MRS SNELLGROVE: I'm all right, Mister . . . have you seen our Alfred?

REPORTER: Yes . . . he's making his way home to Fisher Street.

MRS SNELLGROVE: Good. I'll catch him up. Thanks.

REPORTER: Mrs Snellgrove . . . be careful . . . you know things are bad . . . there's hardly a house standing in Fisher Street.

MRS SNELLGROVE: Oh my God! . . . Oh my God! . . . Is the fire station? . . .

REPORTER: I'm sorry, Mrs Snellgrove . . . should I come with you?

MRS SNELLGROVE: Winnie was in the house . . . on her own . . .

REPORTER: I'll come with you.

[*Fade to . . .*]

Scene xv

[*At the First Aid Station.*]

BERT: I'm looking for my sister, Molly and her friend, Louise . . . Molly Snellgrove . . . I'm Bert Snellgrove . . . Have you seen them, Constable?

CONSTABLE: There's hundreds of people missing at this moment, sir. Just keep calm, sir. The Army Medical Corps has been brought in here to help out. If they've been injured they'll be directed here anyway . . . the hospitals are very busy as you can imagine.

SERGEANT [*whispering to* CONSTABLE]: Don't get in to any detail, son. This is a right mess I can tell you. It'll take weeks to sort this lot out . . . Constable Wordsworth has just wheeled in four bodies . . . well, not really four . . . two hadn't any arms or legs . . . he just stood there crying . . . a grown man crying . . .

BERT: Excuse me, Sergeant . . . is it possible for me to go to my home . . . in Fisher Street?

SERGEANT: The army has put a cordon round the area . . . nobody is allowed in till they've sorted something out. Everything's under control. Nobody can get through . . . and there's not much they could do if they did. Has that head wound been attended to, sir?

BERT: Pardon?

SERGEANT: Your head is bleeding, sir. May I have a look? You'd better have a dressing on it, sir. You've been cut on the scalp.

BERT: Perhaps the safe did it.

SERGEANT: The safe?

BERT: I'm a wages clerk at Gutta Percha, next door to Brunner Mond. I saw the fire as I was packing up for the day . . . Friday is pay day and I'd been cashing up. I was on my way out when I saw the fire . . . so I dashed back and opened the safe hoping to get the money away before anything happened.

SERGEANT: You were too late?

BERT: It blew me head first into the safe. That's probably when I was cut.

SERGEANT: I'll keep an eye out for your sister . . . is Molly her name?

BERT: That's right . . . Molly Snellgrove.

SERGEANT: Now don't you try getting back home, sir. We'll tell you when you can return . . . there could be all kinds of problems in the immediate vicinity of the explosion. It's no place for civilians . . . it's a military matter at the moment.

[*Fade to . . .*]

Scene xvi

[*The* SNELLGROVE *house.*]

SOLDIER: Halt! . . . who goes there? . . . Halt!

ALFRED: Could you give me a hand, soldier? It's my sister . . . I found her laying at the back of our house. She's still breathing, but it's her back.

SOLDIER: Just a minute, son. Don't move her. I'll get some more help. [*exits up the road*]

ALFRED [*talking to* WINNIE]: Winnie . . . Winnie . . . can you hear me? . . . It's me – Alfred . . . Winnie . . .

WINNIE: There was this big wind came right through the house.

ALFRED: Winnie – it's me, Alfred . . .

WINNIE: Alfred . . . Alfred, my back hurts but I'm all right in my head . . . I can't move my arms . . .

ALFRED: Don't try anything fancy . . . a soldier has gone for help.

WINNIE: I've left my letter and my diary in the back room upstairs, Alfred.

ALFRED: Don't worry . . .

WINNIE: If I go to hospital . . . will you look after them?

ALFRED: Of course. Now keep quiet and still.

SOLDIER [*returning*]: There's an orderly and two soldiers coming with a stretcher. Let's get her onto this mattress . . .

[*They lift her gently onto the mattress.*]

ALFRED: Is that more comfortable? . . . Winnie . . . is that more comfortable?

SOLDIER: Don't worry, son . . . she's lapsed into unconsciousness . . . they all do that . . . it's the shock you see . . .

ALFRED: Sure?

SOLDIER: Yeah . . . they all do it.

[*Fade to . . .*]

Scene xvii

[*At the First Aid Station.*]

WOMAN: Somebody called out 'It'll go up – take cover'. I rushed upstairs and brought the kids downstairs and we all hid under the table. There was this loud bang and a kind of wind blowing . . . and the whole bleedin' house fell in . . . We was all all right, I'm just cold, but the kids was really scared I can tell you.

BERT: Molly . . . Molly . . . over here . . . Is that Louise you've got with you?

MOLLY: Oh Bert . . . Bert . . . am I pleased to see you . . . give us a hand with Louise. She's all in.

LOUISE: Thank God we made it . . . God Almighty, I don't want to live through that again!

MOLLY: How's Mum and Elsie? Any news of my Dad?

BERT: There's no news of anybody . . . and I can't find out because they won't let anybody near our street.

MOLLY: There was only our Winnie at home. Me and Louise just worked it out as we was walking here. Our Elsie has got to meet Bill at Victoria . . . he's coming home on sick leave . . . some sick leave I must say . . . let's hope she's got enough sense to take him to his aunt's in Manor Park . . . Alfred was at the Sunday School party . . . our Mum was in Forest Gate and Grandad had a Bowling Club Meeting in Valentines Park, Ilford.

BERT: She'll be all right . . . she's a bright girl . . . she'll be able to look after herself . . . don't worry . . . she'll probably write it all down and send us a letter each. Anyway, what happened to you? Did the explosion damage the Flour Mills?

MOLLY: Nearly demolished it.

LOUISE: We're lucky to be here at all, son. It was very near . . . very near . . .

MOLLY: It was like this . . . Louise and me was working in the kitchen – the kitchen to the canteen at Millenium Mills. We was getting ready . . . getting ready to go home like. Well . . . there was this bloody great bang . . . a ball of fire shot through the air and landed in the Millenium works where people escaped by the grain chutes into the river. Some of 'em couldn't swim. There were three explosions – the buildings fell just like a pack o' cards – killing lots of women. I was knocked unconscious wasn't I, Louise?

LOUISE: Yes, that's right dear . . . it was nearly 9 o'clock when we got out.

BERT: That's nearly two hours.

MOLLY: Well, we was trapped, ya see . . . my little mate Helen . . . well, Nellie we called her for short . . . she had beautiful hair. I can see it now . . . beautiful it was . . . well, it was so long – her hair – she could sit on it. Well, she was sat next to me when it all happened. [*pause*] An iron bar of some sort fell on us . . . I was lucky and I fell between the benches you see . . . and when I looked up she was dead. She didn't suffer anything . . . one moment she was here . . . next she was in paradise . . . the iron bar caught her across the neck. She wore a beautiful expression on her face . . . very peaceful it was . . . very peaceful.

LOUISE: That's true, very true . . . she looked lovely. Mind you, it was all a bit strange. There was all this noise and then no noise at all. We could hear an occasional dripping sound, but just silence . . . nothing.

MOLLY: I could hear somebody breathing . . . very gently . . . breathing in and out, in and out . . . then it stopped . . . and then just silence.

LOUISE: And this dripping sound.

MOLLY: Well, we waited and waited and waited . . . but nobody come . . . I suppose they were too busy. Anyway, our factory wasn't the one that had gone up. I suppose they didn't think to look in our direction. So I says, 'Come on, gel, this won't do – we'll have to help ourselves,' I says. [*The two women begin to act the event. They both stand up.*]

LOUISE: So we started to feel around. We had to be very careful – one wrong move and it might all come down on us.

MOLLY: I cottons on to a big metal beam, so I says, 'Come on, gel, we'll lift this and see what happens.'

LOUISE: We had to be ever so careful though. I cut myself on jagged edges in several places, didn't I, Molly?

MOLLY: Yeah. Well, anyway, we lifts it a bit and there's a God Almighty clattering of wreckage, but it did the trick. We could see a bit of light and we starts to sort of slide on our back underneath the benches. It gets a bit lighter – probably from the fires still burning. And we reaches the outside – well, a window actually on the top floor. So I looks out and it's a hell of a drop. Then I sees this guttering.

LOUISE: So we edges along the guttering – clutching it with our hands. You daren't look down. [LOUISE *gets very upset and begins to shake as she remembers.*] She's much stronger than I am . . . I couldn't hold it . . . I couldn't hold on any longer.

MOLLY: You've got to . . . you've got to . . . Louise.

[LOUISE *stands up and acts the event.*]

LOUISE: I can't – I can't – Oh God – Oh God – I'm going to fall. Molly! Molly!

MOLLY: Give us your wrist, quick! [*She catches* LOUISE*'s wrist.* MOLLY *grabs* LOUISE *and* BERT *wraps a blanket round her and hugs her.*]

LOUISE [*quietly*]: We climbed down.

MOLLY: Fell down more like it. We had a bit of a rest and still nobody came. We thought, well we'd better make our way out. We began walking towards Canning Town. That's when we started meeting people – all walking very slowly – some carrying children. Only stretcher cases could be helped – we were the walking wounded. I took off me petticoat and wound it round my head. When I got home I was taken to a friend who was a nurse – she took me straight to hospital. There was this old lady in the next bed who watched 'em bring me in and settle me down. When they'd finished she looked across and said, 'You're not so bad as me, love' – and then she died.

[*Fade to . . .*]

Scene xviii

[*At the hospital.*]

ORDERLY [*shouting*]: Silvertown casualties, Wards 3 and 4! Report to reception desk and give your names. The nurse has a list. Don't get upset if your relative is not on the list – they could be at the First Aid Station or on their way here – or even at another hospital.

MRS SNELLGROVE: I'm Mrs Snellgrove.

GRANDAD: I'm her father.

MRS SNELLGROVE: Quiet, Dad!

GRANDAD: We're looking for Fireman Snellgrove – Arthur Snellgrove – and my grand-daughter, Winnie Snellgrove.

MRS SNELLGROVE: She's twelve.

NURSE: Snellgrove . . . A fireman you say.

MRS SNELLGROVE: Leading Fireman – Silvertown Fire Station.

NURSE: Could you wait in the room over there, please? . . . Room 3. I'll get the doctor to come and see you in a moment.

GRANDAD: Is he here then?

NURSE: Just wait over in Room 3, please.

MRS SNELLGROVE: Let's do as we're told, Dad. They're all very busy here . . . they know what they're doing . . . now come on . . . Room 3 she said.

[*They enter the room and* GRANDAD *closes the door.* ALFRED *is sitting there.*]

ALFRED: Hallo, Mum . . . Grandad.

MRS SNELLGROVE: Oh, Alfred . . . Alfred . . . thank God! . . .

GRANDAD: Good lad . . . good lad . . . I'm real pleased to see you, son. We heard the Sunday School was done in but you'd got out of it. Are you all right?

ALFRED: I found our Winnie.

MRS SNELLGROVE: Found her? Where?

ALFRED: She was lying in the yard at the back of our house – or what was left of it.

MRS SNELLGROVE: She's all right isn't she?

ALFRED: This soldier and some of his mates brought her here on a mattress. She was unconscious . . . so the soldier said.

MRS SNELLGROVE: Oh Dad . . . Oh Dad . . . she's dying – she's real bad.

GRANDAD: Now just you buck up . . . hold yourself together. Alfred's here . . . I'm here . . . we can see this through . . . mark my words . . . we're tough in Fisher Street . . . now come on, gel. Here's the nurse.

[*The door opens and the* NURSE *enters.*]

NURSE: Please sit down, Mrs Snellgrove. [*she does*]

GRANDAD: I'll stand if you don't mind, nurse.

ALFRED: I'll stand with him too . . . with you, Grandad.

NURSE: It's been a terrible night, Mrs Snellgrove – a terrible night – for lots of people.

MRS SNELLGROVE: Tell me the news, nurse . . . please.

NURSE: I'm afraid your husband, Arthur Snellgrove, was killed outright in the explosion. I don't have all the details . . . the police will supply those in due course. I've also just confirmed your daughter Winnie dead . . . she'd broken her back. Had she lived she would have been a cripple for life I'm afraid.

MRS SNELLGROVE [*weeps*]: What am I going to tell the girls!

GRANDAD [*to* ALFRED]: No nonsense, young Alfred. Take your mother's arm.

NURSE: I'm very, very sorry, Mrs Snellgrove. I advise you to see your own doctor as a precaution . . . he might give some sleeping medicine, should you need it.

GRANDAD: That's all right, nurse. We knows the chemist in Manor Park. He'll fix her up with something. Come on, gel . . . they're busy people.

NURSE: We'll keep the deceased in the mortuary till your undertaker arranges the funeral.

MRS SNELLGROVE: Thank you, nurse. I'm sure you did your best.

ALFRED: Don't worry, mother . . . I'll take me Dad's place . . . just like Stanley Coster does.

[*Entire cast walk on, in single file, from both side of the stage. The* JOURNALIST *takes a central position and begins the song.*]

STOP ME FROM DREAMING

There's been a disaster in Silvertown.
Sixty-nine people all cut down
And two men of the fire brigade
The Brunner Mond dynamite factory
Will go down in history
Long enough for the world to care.

Chorus The Generals they played chess with men's lives.
The government sent words to their wives.
Stop me from dreaming,
I've done it too long.
Stop me from dreaming,
Tell me I'm wrong.
Stop me from dreaming.

Instrumental

Stop me from dreaming,
I've done it too long.
Stop me from dreaming,
Tell me I'm wrong.
Stop me from dreaming.

Packages of death sent on their way,
A million shots fired in a day,
Gifts of death to all mankind.

You children and widows prepare for a fight,
Beware of the men who defend your rights
With the slogan, the song and the gun.

Stop me from dreaming . . . etc.

Scene xix

[*At Victoria Station. All the cast who have sung the song become people at the station.*]

ELSIE [*walking quickly, asking people for the platform for the Folkestone train. She sees the* PORTER *and goes up to him as he is carrying cases for a well-dressed lady*]: Folkestone train arrived?

POSH LADY: Do you mind? [*to* PORTER] Thank you, my man. Could you give them to my driver? He's just over there. [*She takes a mirror from her handbag and adjusts her hat and hair. She sees* ELSIE *staring at her.*] What are you staring at?

ELSIE: Sorry. Sorry. I was just admiring your coat.

POSH LADY: Too pricey for you, sweetie.

ELSIE: You can say that again. Must have cost a fortune.

POSH LADY: Quite. [*She puts the mirror back in her handbag.*] Are you waiting for the Folkestone train too?

ELSIE: Yes, I am. My brother-in-law . . . he's been wounded . . . not badly . . . but they're sending him home. I'm meeting him 'cos his wife – that's my sister – is working late shift you see.

POSH LADY: I see.

ELSIE: Are you?

POSH LADY: I beg your pardon?

ELSIE: Are you waiting for someone?

POSH LADY: That's why I'm standing here . . . I'm waiting for a soldier. A friend of my son's. [PORTER *enters, carrying cases.*] What time is the Folkestone train due to arrive, my man?

PORTER: Folkestone train due here around 7.30, madam. Can't guarantee good timing in the war. [*turning to* ELSIE] Boyfriend from France coming home, eh?

ELSIE: Brother-in-law. Been injured . . . but not too bad. In the Infantry. He's got sick leave.

PORTER: He should be here in five or six minutes. Best of luck. Bad do out in the docks, eh?

ELSIE: Pardon?

PORTER: The explosion . . . in the East End . . . some sort of Government Works . . . blown up.

ELSIE: What name did they give it?

PORTER: They mentioned Silvertown.

ELSIE: Oh my God! My sister worked there till a few weeks ago.

PORTER: Lucky her . . . and you. Here's your Folkestone train. It's almost on time.

ELSIE [*to* POSH LADY]: If she's killed . . . what will I tell her husband? Oh my God. [*She sits down.*] Oh my God. Not our Molly.

[*People come from the Folkestone train. The* POSH LADY *is looking for someone.* BILL, *walking with the aid of a stick, limps through the ticket barrier. The* POSH LADY *goes to meet him. They shake hands.* ELSIE *stands, surprised, a little way off.*]

BILL: You are Harry's mother?

POSH LADY: Yes I am. I was told you had a few of his . . .

BILL: Yes. Yes, I have. [*He hands over a packet of letters, some photographs, a cigarette case.*] Oh, and this. I think he would have liked you to have it. [*He hands her the St Christopher medal.*]

POSH LADY: A St Christopher medal . . . but he wasn't a Catholic.

BILL: I think he'd like you to have it.

POSH LADY: Well . . . yes . . . well . . . Thank you.

[ELSIE *interrupts by putting her arms around him.*]

ELSIE: Come on. Come on, Bill . . . never mind her. There's been an explosion down our end. Your Molly could be in it.

BILL: Oh God . . . no . . . no . . . not that.

[*They exit.*]

Scene xx

[*At the newspaper office.* REPORTER *has just come in from the Coroner's Court, where the bodies have been identified.*]

REPORTER: Look . . . I've got a big problem here. Just listen to my notes . . . how am I going to write this lot up?

EDITOR: Don't bellyache – read it out.

REPORTER: 'PC Hugget – On approaching the scene of the explosion I came across Stephen Arthur Jepson, engine driver. He appeared to be suffering from injuries to the legs and thighs. I tied up the legs as best I could with some handkerchiefs. I carried the deceased towards Post Police Station. On the way I found a wheelbarrow and put him in it. When I got to the hospital, first aid was rendered, but as the hospital was full I took him to another institution, where he passed away.

'Ernest Parks. Occupation – Gas Worker. Address . . . I live in Greenwich, yer Honour. Who do you identify? . . . My brother-in-law, Edgar Wenborn. Coroner . . . How do you identify him? Ernest Parks . . . I identify the foot by the boot and sock and from the fact that a piece of the Providential Almanac has been put in the boot to ease it.' See what I mean – how can I report that?

EDITOR: Just carry on – I'll tell you what to print.

REPORTER: People queued up to identify the dead – there's over sixty people have been killed in the explosion or have died subsequently. [*reading his notes*] 'Henry Pottinger identified the manager of licensed premises. Mrs Hopkins identified her son. An unknown child identified his grandad, a fruit salesman. And one woman identified her husband, a fireman, and her daughter.'

EDITOR: Right. I can see you're very upset. Look, laddie, we'll have to have the details of the fireman's widow, but in the meantime I've written a few paragraphs for Saturday's edition – just look through it and see if it sounds right.

REPORTER: Any tea?

EDITOR: Have mine . . . it was made ten minutes ago.

REPORTER: Thanks. [*He now reads aloud the* EDITOR*'s paragraphs.*] 'Stratford Park Gazette – 27 January 1917. The Great Tragedy which has befallen the people of East London this week has, for the time being, over-shadowed every other question. Even the war has been forgotten for the time being, except insofar as it was realised that the explosion was but a wider issue of the great convulsion which has rent Europe during the past two years.

'As to the cause of the explosion, we can only say that the Government has promised an inquiry and it is in the interests of all concerned that the inquiry should be as searching and complete as it is possible to make it. The explosion was heard not only all over London and the Home Counties, but in places as far away as the North of Cambridgeshire and Norfolk.

'About 7 o'clock last night a fire started at a factory in the East End of London, near the river, which was employed in refining explosives. Fortunately, a few moments elapsed after the commencement of the fire before the explosion occurred, during which many of the operators were able to escape. The factory was completely destroyed. Three rows of houses in the immediate vicinity were practically demolished.' But what about the people . . . what about the people . . . houses, streets, factories, churches, shops . . . all blown to pieces, and the people with them? And we know quite a few of them . . . we've done our features on them . . . we've got their photographs – remember? Smiling . . . with their arms folded . . . outside their houses . . . and now. . . . and now what . . . for those who survive . . . what do they survive on? Handouts? Just look at this letter . . . are you going to print it?

EDITOR: Of course . . . it's addressed to the Mayor.

REPORTER [*reading*]: 'Dear Mr Mayor, I am sure you will wish to make known in the locality the gracious messages and generous donations in aid of the sufferers received from their Majesties the King and Queen and from Her Majesty Queen Alexandra which were announced in the national press today.' Then there's this list of donations:

King – £250
Queen – £100
Queen Alexandra – £100
Princess Royal – £50
William Cory & Son – £525 – Well done, lads
N M Rothschild & Sons – £105

'These monies will be applied only to exceptional cases.' Exceptional cases . . . who's going to decide that? Which bloody clerk is going to step forward and decide whether a fireman's widow or the widow of a publican who's had his head blown off is . . . an exceptional case? It's bloody starting already. The creeping paralysis of officialdom is spinning an instant web of forms, questions and conditions. Haven't they suffered enough? Look at this item for Saturday's edition: 'The emergency committee have been tracing missing children and their parents – more than 100 little ones have been found. Seven children in the hospital have not been claimed and it is feared they have been orphaned by this terrible explosion.' Are they exceptional cases . . . are they? And who's to blame for this lot . . . who's going to carry the responsibility?

EDITOR: The Official Secrets Act will . . .

REPORTER: Will obliterate all the evidence and cover up all the guilty . . . and who is going to pay? The King and Queen won't rebuild Silvertown – so who will?

[*Fade to . . .*]

Scene xxi

[*At the First Aid Station.*]

1ST WOMAN: It's wiped out our street – all the bloody lot.

2ND WOMAN: Could have been worse.

1ST WOMAN: How *could* it have been worse, you silly cow.

2ND WOMAN: You could have been in it.

1ST WOMAN: We bloody well was in it . . . have you been affected, love? . . . Nurse . . . nurse . . . get this lady a cup of hot sweet tea. I think she's roaming in the head.

1ST MAN: A big girder . . . reckon it weighed over a ton . . . came through the roof and fell on our bedstead. That was lucky 'cos it meant the front room ceiling only collapsed slowly so as we could get out.

2ND MAN: Did you see that dead horse . . . on its side all bloated like? And another thing . . . you had to laugh . . . there was a wall still standing behind that Belgium lady's house and she had a few hens . . . well these were calm as you like, still sitting. They laid five eggs . . . they was taken to the relief kitchen.

1ST MAN: Course mouth almighty Donovan – him what serves behind the bar at the Abbey Arms – God he's a liar . . . he reckons he went down the yard to relieve himself and the explosion lifted him and blew him out of the toilet. He ended up flat on his face in the yard still holding the paper in his hand.

2ND MAN: Could've happened I suppose . . . somebody was bound to be relieving themselves when it happened.

1ST MAN: Yes . . . but not bloody Donovan.

2ND MAN: I hear the Snellgroves caught it. Two of 'em are dead. That young Alfred apparently got through the cordon of soldiers and found his sister Winnie dying.

1ST MAN: Nice girl – took to writing letters. She wrote one to Bill Smithers asking him to stop using his saw-mill in school time or get it oiled. It made a hell of a racket . . . 'none of her bloody business' he said. He didn't reply.

1ST WOMAN: That ignorant git . . . he didn't reply 'cos he can't . . . he can't read a word and he can't write his name. By the way, the Mayor's coming in half an hour.

1ST MAN: Wonder if there's going to be a handout . . . I'm skint . . . all my money was in the house.

1ST WOMAN: I'll be saying that too . . . all my jewels was there as well . . . got from the Duchess of Devonshire for helping her with her washing . . . worth a fortune . . . [*she laughs*] all blown up in the explosion.

[*Letter from Mayor read by* REPORTER *whilst next scene is set.*]

'Mayor's Parlour, January 1917. On the early morning of Saturday I attended the scene with our MP, Alderman Thorne, and there met Dr Addison, the Minister for Munitions. We consider it quite unnecessary to make a public appeal. The emergency committee and their wonderful lady workers have so far made sure that no one goes hungry or without temporary shelter. The catastrophe is the result of war and the Government are prepared to foot the bill. I move a vote of thanks and appreciation to the Emergency Committee. Signed: His Worship the Mayor.'

[*After the letter, the children sing:*]

Poor Winnie she's a-grieving, a-grieving, a-grieving,
Poor girlie she's a-grieving on a cold winter's day.
She wrote a little letter, a letter, a letter
To say what she was thinking down Silvertown way.
But nobody was listening, was listening, was listening,
But nobody was listening on a cold winter's day.
So all the shells kept firing, and whining and shining,
And killing all the soldiers, on a cold winter's day.
Now Winnie's gone to heaven, to heaven, to heaven
And Winnie goes to heaven to join them today.

[*Fade to . . .*]

Scene xxii

[*Outside the remains of* FIREMAN SNELLGROVE*'s house. Present:* MRS SNELLGROVE, ELSIE, MOLLY *and* BILL, BERT, LOUISE, ALFRED *and two* SOLDIERS.]

1ST SOLDIER: I'll have to stand here and supervise.

BILL: What for?

1ST SOLDIER: Because you're only allowed to take your belongings and there's been looting during the night. One of my mates took a shot at one of them. A fella turned up this morning with a horse and cart asking could he collect scrap metal.

MRS SNELLGROVE: Come on, let's get on with it. Molly . . . Elsie . . . you look for drawers with clothes in . . . I'll scrub around for a bit of bedding. Them oak chest of drawers will be under this lot. Alfred . . . you get kitchen utensils and Bill and Bert . . . anything you find you think useful.

MOLLY: Are you sure you're all right, Mum? Wouldn't you be better off at Aunt Ada's?

MRS SNELLGROVE: Look Molly, just get on with it. My Arthur wouldn't want me to hang around moaning . . . the family has got to be sorted . . . and we've got to get a house.

BERT: Come on, Bill, let's see what we can salvage.

BILL: Well, there's the old piano – no front on it – does it play?

BERT [*fingering a few notes*]: Not bad, but slightly out of tune.

BILL: We've only got a handcart . . . I don't think it's a priority, do you?

ALFRED: There's nothing left of the kitchen. The whole house must have fallen that way. It's under tons of bricks.

MOLLY: Come on, Louise . . . there aren't any short cuts . . . let's start moving bricks.

LOUISE: Are you sure your mother's all right, kid? I mean, you've just lost your Dad and your sister.

MOLLY: None of us really realises it yet . . . Just keep removing them bricks . . . It's something to do. When we have the funeral next week, that's when it will really hit her . . . and me too . . . so come on, Louise, let's get at it . . . let's attempt to get some sense out of this mess.

BILL [*shouting*]: I've found the kitchen table . . . it looks all right.

MRS SNELLGROVE: Get it out . . . we can always polish it up.

LOUISE: There's a big cupboard over here, Molly.

MOLLY: What's in it?

LOUISE: Just a minute . . . have you got a stick?

MOLLY: There's enough timber here to start a bonfire, Louise . . . here, grab this.

MRS SNELLGROVE [*shouting*]: Alfred . . . just you be careful! Don't go too near the far wall . . . it could collapse any minute . . . just pick up what you can find and load it on the cart.

ALFRED: All right, Mum.

BERT: I've found the toilet.

LOUISE: You would . . . you've got that kind of mind. Always been a vulgar streak in young Bert, have you noticed, Molly?

MOLLY: What's in the cupboard . . . have you opened it yet?

LOUISE: Coats and wellingtons.

ALFRED: Winnie's desk should be over here by the back door somewhere. Her room was right over the kitchen. [*He begins to move bricks.*]

BILL: Can I give you a hand, Alfred?

ALFRED: Winnie had a small set of drawers by her bed. Her books and diaries were in it. I wouldn't want them destroyed or read by the workmen when they clear up. They was private, you see.

BILL: All right. Let's have a go. [*They begin to move the rubble.*] What colour were they? Dark brown or light brown, like oak?

ALFRED: It was painted white, like plywood.

BILL: Is this it?

ALFRED: Let's have a look . . . yes . . . I think that's the top of it. It looks smashed up. Let's take it out a piece at a time.

BILL [*calling*]: Soldier! Soldier! Could you give us a hand here to get these drawers out?

SOLDIER: Just hold my rifle, son. [*He gives the rifle to* ALFRED.]

ALFRED: Is it loaded? [*He begins to examine it – he's lost all interest in the chest of drawers.*]

SOLDIER: I wouldn't give it to you if it was.

BERT: Too true, mate. A lad like that might run off to France with it and win the war single-handed.

[ALFRED *points the gun and pretends to shoot and bayonet invisible enemies. He kneels down and shoots and then he lies full stretch and fires.*]

MOLLY [*in anger on seeing Alfred with the gun*]: What the hell's going on here then? Haven't you had enough of war for one week, soldier? I suppose you're setting up our Alfred for the slaughter too aren't ya? Well, get that bloody gun off him and do whatever it is you're supposed to do and leave our Alfred out of it. Bert, I'm surprised at you.

BILL: But he was only . . .

MOLLY [*shouting*]: Take that bloody weapon off our Alfred!

BILL: Give it here, Alfie . . . give the soldier a hand. Come and have a drink from my flask, love. Come on.

SOLDIER: Well, there you are, son. There's only two drawers intact. The rest got smashed up.

ALFRED [*looking in the drawers*]: That's all right. I can see what I want. There's her exercise books and that's the paper she used for writing letters. Look, here's her last piece of writing in her diary.

SOLDIER: What does it say?

ALFRED: Diaries are private, Winnie always said.

SOLDIER: Well, I'm a stranger, son. I won't tell anybody. I don't know anybody to tell.

ALFRED: All right. But you promise you won't tell the newspapers or anything?

SOLDIER: On my soldier's honour.

ALFRED: Right . . . Sunday . . . that's last Sunday . . . the day before this happened, Sunday 16 January, 1917. It's written like a poem.

SOLDIER: That's all right. I don't mind.

ALFRED [*reading*]:

'Dear God, each night I pray
You'll stop this war and make men say
That fighting, bloodshed, grief and tears
Have no place in our coming years.

I lie awake and hear the sound
Of shells being filled at Brunner Mond.
A German mother now knows well
The sadness of a Silvertown shell.'

Then it stops being poetry and goes on to ordinary writing.

SOLDIER: I see . . . carry on.

ALFRED [*still reading*]: 'Yesterday, Saturday, I heard the kids playing in the street. They were playing "Ring a Ring of Roses". Mr Sadler, our teacher, told us this was a song about the plague in Britain hundreds of years ago, when thousands of people died. They knew they had the plague by this rose-shaped scab on their arms or legs. And the sneeze part, "atishoo, atishoo, all fall down" meant they all died. I was very fed up by the whole thing, and I'm fed up with this war. The papers was full again last week of soldiers from West Ham who had been killed in the war. I know something dreadful is going to happen to us . . . I'm sure Brunner Mond will destroy us, but who listens to Winnie Snellgrove age 14. Must write a letter to the Prime Minister. Perhaps he'll stop it.

Ring a Ring a Roses
Atishoo, Atishoo,
We all fall down.'

BERT: Don't you ever repeat any of that, soldier.

SOLDIER: I won't . . . I won't.

BERT: Just look at this place . . . flattened . . . reduced to rubble. A whole street life destroyed in the fraction of a second.

SOLDIER: Same as France.

BERT: Aye, soldier. The war came to Silvertown. It's just like the Somme, soldier. Just like the Somme.

[*Full cast sings:*]

DEAR GENERALS

Dear Generals, I wish you could see
All the destruction that lies around me.
Why does this happen? Why is this so?
I need to know.

I'll write you a letter
But you won't reply.
Your cosy life's sheltered,
You can't hear the cries
Of innocent children,
Of widowed young wives,
You close your eyes.

Dear Generals, what did you gain?
Where is the glory in so much pain?
Where is the victory
For those who have died?
It's hollow, dear generals,
You destroy lives.

[*During the song, the following letters are read:*]

Dockers' Sympathy

The following is copy of resolution passed by the Executive Council of the Dock, Wharf, Riverside and General Workers' Union at its meeting just concluded:

East London Explosion

This Executive Council of the Dock, Wharf, Riverside and General Workers' Union offers its condolences to the bereaved of those destroyed by the East London explosion, many of whom were members of the above Union.

This Executive is of the opinion that the manufacture of high explosives should in every case be isolated and not carried on in thickly populated districts.

We also regret the loss of the resources to the country, and trust the workers employed at other factories will concentrate their efforts to prevent any diminution in total output.

We trust an immediate enquiry into the matter will be instituted and that ample compensation will be provided thc relatives of the victims.

Clerk to the Council
Ministry of Munitions of War
6 Whitehall Place SW1
20 December 1917

Dear Mr Thorne

With reference to the deputation which I received from the West Ham Corporation regarding compensation in respect of the Silvertown Explosion. I am writing to say that the

Department have been in further communication with the Treasury on the subject of the claims made by the Corporation for loss of rates and the loss of revenue in respect of their Electricity Undertaking.

The matter having been fully considered by Mr Winston Churchill with the Lords Commissioners of His Majesty's Treasury – they see no reason for modifying the previous decision that the claim was not one which the Ministry could entertain.

THE END